<u>371 Guidelines to</u>
<u>Kriya Practitioners</u>

Based on guidelines given by

Yogiraj Rev.Shyamacharan Lahiri,

Yogacharya Rev.Panchanan Bhattachraya

and other Kriya Yogis

Foreword

It is a testimony to the Divine Grace of Shri Shri Lahiri Mahashaya that the 1st edition of this book has been well received by devotees all over the world. The entire effort has been due to the Grace of my Master - Paramhansa Yogananda, at whose Lotus Feet I dedicate the present 2nd edition of the book as well.

<u>108 Words of Wisdom by Shri Shri Lahiri Mahashaya, has been added in this 2nd Edition from His personal diaries.</u> Hoping & Praying that this words of Lahiri Baba will help the devotees in his/her Sadhana. And may all sincere seekers of God reach at highest level of consciousness, where Mahavtar Babaji, Lahiri Baba, Sri Yukteshwarji, Yoganandaji and all Great Gurus reigns. (Here Point No.12,13,14,15 and 88 is of Khechari Mudra and Talabya Kriya to be noted.)

Typographical error has been rectified at some places and fonts has been enlarged for easy reading. All Proper Sanskrit Slokas and Words are now correctly typed in this 2nd edition.

Kriya-Yoga Sadhaka Samhita

(Guidelines to Kriya-Practitioners)

Atmakarma (Kriya Yoga)

Preface

No rules are applicable to a yogi who has become one with Brahma and is immersed in eternal bliss. Whatever he says or does takes the form of rules. Such rules are free from any human error. A great sadhak not only keeps on performing his sadhana but he also gives some guidelines for the upcoming generation of sadhakas. The guidelines help the new sadhakas and sadhikas to find an answer to their queries & clear away the clouds of doubts.

It was not possible to repeatedly answer various questions of sadhakas & sadhikas. Therefore keeping in view their need & request, this booklet containing the sermons of legendary *Yogiraj Rev. Shyama charan Lahiri, Yogacharya Rev. Panchanan Bhattacharya, Yogashri Rev. Shrish Mukherjee & Yogivar Rev. Gurudev Nitaicharan Banerjee* has been published. May God bless those generous people who have helped in the publication of this booklet.

Hope, this booklet will be of immense help to all of you in Atmayoga. (Spiritual Practice.)

Atmakarma (Kriya-yoga)

Regular visits to temples or mosques or churches; offering prayers, chanting hymns, shouting holy verses from Koran singing of devotional songs or bhajans etc. cannot be regarded as tools for devotion (Bhakti) since these are incapable of mitigating the traumas which plague human beings. People performing all these religious gymnastics are deprived of peace.

Devotion means unconditional surrender before the Almighty. When a seeker forgets himself i.e. when a seeker loses his mind and comes face to face with God all around as a result of Kriya-practice, devotion is said to have been perfected. When complete secrecy is maintained in respect of devotion, it bears fruit. The true and incorruptible devotion (devotion to only one) is without a goal. Where there is devotion, there is divinity (God). Where there is kriya- practice, peace prevails there.

As we Know, prana (breathing) is the basic element of our body. Without prana the body becomes corpse , a burden even for the loved ones who are in a hurry to bury or arrange for the funeral. Thus we exist because of prana. In a normal human body normal breathing count goes upto 21,600 during 24 hours. As we breathe , the age of our body decreases.

There is a slight pause between inhaling and exhaling but it is not experienced by a normal human being because his focus of attention is far away from breathing (prana). If the mind focuses on prana (breathing), one can enter the eternal and supernatural infinite world within the human body. The spiritual reality is revealed only to them who reach this world . It is not possible to delve deep into this wonderful world just by reading or listening about it.

The worshippers of prana automatically get the four basic things of life i.e artha (wealth), dharma [Right way], kama [Needs] and moksha (liberation).

The worshippers of prana (those who regulate their breathing) need to learn this art of worship (regulation of prana) from Rev. Gurudeva. This art is called 'Atmakarma' i.e the Kriya-yoga. It cannot be practiced by seeing, listening or reading. By trying to do so, one is prone to suffering.

Therefore it must be learnt from a qualified trainer (one who is Atmastha) by surrendering to Him or Her, considering Him or Her to be above all. The internal pranayama forming the core of this practice can lead the practitioner to the status of 'siddhavastha' if regular practice with devotion is undertaken.

This pranayama is of three types : (1) lower (Adhama) (2) Mediocre (Madhyama) & (3) Pure (Uttam). With Guru's blessings a seeker is able to practice pure pranayams but he has to start with lower pranayama. Internal pranayama is a special type of pranayama which symbolizes ascent and descent of prana through six chakras in the spinal cord.

The practice of Atmakarma must be undertaken under the close supervision of Rev. Gurudeva. The Rev.Gurudeva who initiates a seeker into Atmakarma and supervises kriya-practice later on must have attained the tranquil state after kriya i.e he must be Atmastha, he must be a symbol of renunciation and always remain in the state of chaitanya samadhi.

He also must be in a position to keep his tongue inverted in such a way that none can see his tongue even if he keeps his mouth wide open i.e **'he must have perfected khechari'.** There are certain people who claim to be Guru just because they are descendants of some real (siddha) Guru.

There are others who have learnt wrong method of Kriya and deceive people by misguiding them just for the sake of money. In ancient times our rishis were householders yet self-aware.

In recent times there are frauds masquerading as guru. They put on saffron robes, decorate their forehead with sandal paste with peculiar designs, put on costly garlands and maintain strange hair style just to mislead people and rob them of their hard earned money.

Such people do not have any idea of yoga or mantra. They spread falsehood. They make false speeches by misquoting and misinterpreting religious treatises. The common people are deceived because of their outer appearance. It is, therefore, necessary to be cautious against such people.

Those who have transcended pleasure and pain, gain and loss, victory and defeat, happiness and sorrow, respect and insult, high and low and have attained the state of equanimity by fixation of prana are indeed true gyanis (Wise men). It is sheer luck to meet such gyanis (Atmastha).

The commonly used pranayama which is practiced by closing nostrils in turns is not only incorrect but it may also lead to some disease since it advocates deliberate delaying of exhaling. One must perform spiritual practice in accordance with the rules of nature. Atmakarma (the kriya-yoga) incorporates inner (antarmukhi) pranayama which purifies not only the mind but also the body.

The asana (posture) which helps to concentrate for a longer period of time is most suitable to a seeker. One must proceed on the path of the Kriya-yoga keeping all these facts into consideration. Human beings can attain self-liberation and be free from jeevabhava (identification with body) by following the path of the Kriya-yoga with utmost devotion.

These days most of the people do not know the real meaning of a spiritual practice. Even the idol worship at various places is bogus since the priest is quite unaware of the real method of idol worship. The spiritual books which are faulty or some senior priests who are ignorant guide such priests.

It is for this reason that idol worship has lost its glitter and has become commercialized (a separate business). The priest considers his work as a source of livelihood.

So he does not bother about the right method. We have reached such a dismal state of affairs that even the worship of God has become a means of livelihood. The real meaning of worship is known to these few people who have advanced on the path of Atmakarma (the Kriya-yoga) by practicing internal pranayama and other techniques which form the core of the Kriya- yoga but such saints (mahatmas) are rarely detected by common people since they hide themselves completely even though they live amidst the common folk.

The attempt to understand the real meaning of worship by exploring various mantras with the help of grammar is just useless and waste of time and precious human life.

Our religious treatises (shastras) preach "God dwells in the heart of all beings i.e. God is present everywhere". In spite of being aware of this we fight as Hindus, Muslims, Christians etc. Does the same God not dwell in the heart of Muslims or Christians? Does the God dwell only in the hearts of Hindus? If it is so, then the religious treatises preach wrong things or we commit mistake in their explanation. Our religious treatises are not wrong since they preach the truth i.e. the God is omnipresent.

Indeed we are at fault since we read the religious texts through the lens of selfish ends. These days the ignorant people propagate their own faulty opinion by misquoting religious texts. The plain fact is "we do not have the courage to admit that we do not know or we are ignorant" we are slaves of our minds which should have been otherwise.

We should be masters of our minds. In the absence of Atmakarma (practice of the Kriya- yoga), people have forgotten their real face (the atma) and become slaves of mind.

Therefore the Atmakarma (practice of the Kriya-yoga) is the need of the hour. The Vedas say "जन्मना जयते शूद्रः संस्कारात द्विज उच्चत्ये"॥ (Janmana jayate sudrah, sanskarat dwiza uchyate) i.e. by birth everybody is a sudra, from sanskara one becomes a द्विज (dwiza) (re- birth) i.e. being initiated into Atmakarma or the Kriya- yoga. After that Vedapatha (recital of the Veda) means kriya –practice which leads to the tranquil state after kriya i.e. self- knowledge or knowing Brahma and becoming Brahmana.

<u>Lord Krishna narrates in the Gita-</u>

चातुर्वर्ण्यं मया सृष्टं गुणकर्मविभागशः।
तस्य कर्तारमपि मां विद्ध्यकर्तारमव्ययम्।। 4.13।।

The four varnas (Brahman, Kshatriya, Vaishya and Shudra) have been classified on the basis of gunas and karmas. Though I (God) have created them, I am still beyond the realm of doing i.e. I am Avyaya (beyond destruction) and Akarta (a non-doer). So those who have realized Brahma by performing Atmakarma are the Brahmanas. None can become a Brahmin just by putting on sacred thread and uttering gayatri mantra without knowing its real meaning.

Gorakhnath was born in the caste of milkman, Vishwamitra was a kshatriya by caste, Kabirdas was the son of a weaver and Vashishtha was born from the womb of a prostitute. All of them became well known Brahmins (saints) by practicing Atmakarma (the Kriya-yoga) with devotion.

Gautam samhita incorporates a shloka-

"क्षन्तं दन्तं जितक्रोधां जितात्मनं जितेन्द्रियम्
तमेव ब्राह्मणं मन्ये शेषः शूद्रः इति स्मृतः इति"।

This shloka highlights the following features of a Brahmin : forgiving, controller of sense organs, conqueror of anger and self- realized.

The rest i.e. those who do not possess these features are Shudras. Thus Brahmanas, Kshatriyas , Vaishyas and Shudras etc. are the states of a sadhaka depending on his spiritual progress. It has nothing to do with clan or name. It is a sin to consider them to be the index of social division.

Lord Krishna proclaims in the Gita :

नास्ति बुद्धिरयुक्तस्य न चायुक्तस्य भावना।

न चाभावयतः शान्तिरशान्तस्य कुतः सुखम्।। 2.66 ।।

i.e. those who have not submerged their intellect into brahma have not experienced soul and those who have no acquaintance with soul, have not attained peace (bliss). Those who have not enjoyed the tranquil state, cannot be blissful. One is deprived of this blissful state because of outwardly movements of mind caused by deep-rooted attachments with people and things (object).

It is ,therefore , essential for a seeker to find out a way which can lead to fixation of prana i.e. seize the wavering tendency of mind.

Otherwise the six enemies (lust, anger, greed, attachment (moha), pride (mada) and matsar) will overwhelm the seeker and make him restless. When these enemies attack, no outwardly worship or bhajans can save the worshipper. The outwardly forms of worship (karma kanda) and devotional songs are just incapable of confronting these powerful enemies.

It is, therefore, essential to follow the path of Atmakarma i.e. the Kriya- yoga. It is impossible to overwhelm these enemies without practicing the techniques of the Kriya- yoga, the pranayama being its core. Considering it, practice of the pranayama is the fundamental duty of a seeker.

Yama and niyama are perfected by the practice of the pranayama. There is no other way to perfect yama and niyama.

After practicing sufficient number of pranayamas, the longings will seize which prove that yama and niyama have been perfected. The best sitting posture (asana) for the Kriya-practice is the one which helps in sitting comfortably for a long period of time.

With the regular practice of pure pranayamas one can gradually attain pratyahara, dharana, dhyana, and samadhi. 12 pure pranayamas lead to pratyahar, 144 such pranayamas lead to dharana, 1728 such pranayamas lead to dhyana and 20,736 such pranayamas lead to samadhi. All these can be understood by sitting at the feet of a real guru (Atmastha). The state of dhyana attained as a result of the practice of 1728 pranayamas, leads to the enjoyment of tranquil state after kriya which is a blissful state.

After the practice of 20,736 pure pranayamas, the sadhaka feels to have become one with God (yuktavastha) i.e. being one with brahma. In such a state the sadhaka is completely freed from ego and is not trapped by the disturbances caused by ego-trips. That is the time when the whole universe seems to be replete with soul (atmamaya).

In India there is a common misconception. The people in general consider a saffron-clad or long- curly haired person to be a sanyasi or a saint. It is nothing but sheer non –sense.

Generally it is preached that self-realization is impossible without getting rid of wife, son, household and worldly belongings. In fact there is not even an iota of truth in such a notion. Indeed such preachers consider themselves wiser than the God.

If wife, children and worldly belongings were barriers to self-realization, the God would not have created them at all. These ignorant preachers lose sight of our ancient rishis (seers) who were perfect householders.

Indeed they had attained self-realization through regular practice of atmakriya with devotion but at the same time they continued to perform the duties of an ideal house- holder as well.

Indeed the saffron-clad thugs of recent times are timid, soft-spoken, absconders, irresponsible, work-shirks and luxury-lovers who have nothing to do with spirituality but use it as a tool for personal aggrandizement with worldly belongings which they preach to get rid of. They really have caused great havoc with social morality by misleading the large chunk of innocent people.

Indeed the cause of bondage is our own mind. Sacrifice of worldly things & near and dear ones may be termed as rajasic or tamasic sacrifice. It is worth remembering—World is nothing but longings in different forms .The person who has been able to transcend longings in their various forms is a real sanyasi . His sacrifice is sattwik one but such a person is rarely available.

With regular practice of Atmakarma , physical fitness is ensured at first. After getting rid of diseases a seeker ensures his spriritual progress. Gradually the mind becomes spotless like a mirror which reflects the Brahma all around. Mind stops its wavering tendency and the sadhaka becomes one with the Brahma i.e. attains shivatwa-the qualities of Lord Shiva.

My Gurubaba (Yogiraj Rev. Shyamacharan Lahiri) never permitted anybody to put on a saffron-robe and become sanyasi in the name or form. He even forbade people to use the prefix guru with his name. He always advocated for the practice of Atmakarma i.e. the Kriya-yoga and discouraged karma- kanda (outer form of worship). This Atmakarma must be learnt from those who have been instructed to initiate sadhakas into the Kriya-yoga. Such initiators are Atmastha.

<u>Publication of the techniques of the Kriya-yoga is strictly prohibited because no one can learn it by reading</u>. Even after initiation people find it difficult to practice and, therefore, they have to be in regular touch with their initiators to get their practice checked again and again until and unless they attain a degree of perfection in the Kriya-practice.

This "Atmakarma" is not available to all. One must fulfill eligibility criteria. Those who are not eligible for this practice will not derive positive outcome from its practice. The initiator knows who is eligible for Atmakarma and who is not. It is He who decides by performing certain tests best known to Him/Her.

If a sadhaka keeps on performing Atmakarma regularly with devotion and maintains secrecy about it, he is bound to have self-realization sooner or later. Rev. Lahari Baba used to say "banat, banat bani jayee" which means keep on trying, you will eventually succeed. If one is regular and has devotion for Atmakarma, he or she will undoubtedly have self-realization.

There is not even a shred of doubt in the fact that a seeker attains self-realization (siddhavastha) and liberation (muktavastha) if he/she practices this transcendental karma (Paravidya or Atmakarma i.e. the Kriya-yoga) strictly following the instructions of initiator (the Gurudeva) from the day one. In case one is slack in following these instructions of his initiator (guru) from the day one but keeps on performing Atmakarma more or less correctly, he will improve physically, mentally, economically and have a little bit of mental peace but he cannot have self – realization.

In order to practice Atmakarma one does not have to be away from parents, children , wife , household and worldly belongings. One has to prepare oneself in order to get rid of worldly longings in different forms and remain detached but it is not possible without practicing Atmakarma with patience, perseverance, strong determination and unwavering devotion.

Whatever has been explained above has directly been received from the benevolent Gurudeva. The ability to narrate all that has been stated above is the result of the Kriya- practice and blessings from Rev. Gurudeva. Fixation of prana is the fundamental objective of the Kriya – yoga. This fixed prana is denoted by Shri Krishna or Bhagawan in Shrimad Bhagwadgita.

'प्रानोहि भगवनिषः, प्राणो विष्णुः पितामहः ;
प्राणेन् धर्यते लोकः, सर्व प्राणायाम जगत्।'

The kriya practitioners need not perform any outer form of worship i.e. those who have experienced the God in the form of prana do not bother for any other form of worship. Indeed a person residing in a palace will have no desire to live in a hut .

Commenting on the meaning of the word 'indifferent', my Gurubaba says that only those people are indifferent who have been able to ensure fixation of prana in their head at a specified place. This state is availed of as a result of benediction from Rev. Gurudeva. Generally people take the dictionary meaning of the word indifferent which is close to sadness, outer sacrifice etc.

A yogi is without a choice so he is desireless. As a leaf moves because of wind, so a yogi seems to be performing various worldly activities according to inspirations from the God (Paramatma). A yogi neither wishes for something nor is he against anything. A sadhaka need not be away from wife and family in order to have self – realization. There may be plenty of wealth in the name of a yogi but he will remain detached from it. Such a yogi is the real devotee to the God. Such people are called brave sadhakas.

A sadhaka may remain detached even when he lives in his own household. King Janak is a glaring example to prove this point. It is for this reason that king Janak was called Videh i.e. one who has transcended body though he is still alive and has physical form (body).

Even if a person goes to forest leaving everything behind , he cannot be free from his filthy mind filled with lust, anger, greed, fear and other ailments.

If the mind is not freed from all these diseases caused by attachment to people, objects etc., there is no use leaving everything physically and going to mountains, forests, pilgrimage etc.

So, the house is the best place for Atmakarma. If a sadhaka maintains utmost secrecy and regularly practices Atmakarma with devotion, he will have self-realization sooner or later.

While explaining the mystery of Bhakti (devotion), Lord Krishna says the sadhakas practicing Atmakarma automatically get near to Him and become one with Him.

As a person who has lost his only son does not feel the impact of cold weather even if the temperature has touched the freezing point because of sorrow caused by the loss of his only son, so a yogi immersed in the Brahma (Atmastha) does not feel any sort of agony whether it is physical, mental or bodily.

All these are possible because of regular practice of Atmakarma. Mere reading or listening will be of no avail. It is, therefore, the bounden duty of each human being to engage himself or herself in the regular practice of Atmakarma.

(This essay is based on information provided in the book "Jagat Aur Ami" in Bengali by Rev. Panchanan Bhattacharya, the chief disciple of legendary Rev. Sri Shyama Charan Lahiri Mahashaya. Collection of materials from various pages and its coherent reproduction has been done by Shri Vats Mahodaya).

Guidelines to Kriya - Practitioners :-

1	The fundamental duty of a kriya-practitioner is to regularly perform kriya-practice with devotion.
2	Being in a tranquil (blissful) state after kriya-practice is called samadhi.
3	Kriya practice at 4 o'clock in the morning (4 a.m.) is beneficial for a kriya practitioner.
4	Kriya–practice with devotion on a regular basis leads to attainment of peace. It also sharpens intellect and enhances fame.
5	Parents should be adored like the God.
6	Those who worship "prana" are the gem among common people. The wise are the gem among the Kriya-practitioners.
7	Japa must be performed on each chakra while doing 'omkar kriya'.
8	Those who have become self-absorbed (brahma leena) as a result of vigourous kriya-practice are real Brahmins.
9	The devoted kriya-practitioners who perform kriya-practice regularly are 'kshatriyas'.
10	Those who are not regular with kriya-practice, who make it a business and those who tend to deliver a lecture on kriya-practice are Vaishyas.
11	Those who do not practice kriya regularly are Shudras.
12	Two sittings for kriya-practice in a time-span of 24 hours is necessary for a sincere practitioner.

13	Performing pranayamas on the chakras at the back bone is better than performing pranayamas on the front side.
14	Those who have been able to fix their prana in the 'Kutastha' are real 'Gurus'. Their gospels must be followed in letter and spirit.
15	Those who know Brahma (Brahmin) are able to fix their prana in the Kutastha at will irrespective of their posture (sitting, walking etc.) and the work they are engaged in. They always keep on hearing the sound of 'om'. They see 'uttam purush' in the Kutastha and are self-absorbed (Brahmaleena).
16	Regular perusal of the Gita with commentary by none other than the legendary Yogiraj (published by Arrya mission) and other books dealing with kriya-practice (published by Arrya mission) is of immense help.
17	Patience, devotion, regularity and sincere efforts are pre-requisites of success in the Kriya-practice.
18	A kriya-practitioner must guard himself against ostentation by maintaining confidentiality in respect of kriya-practice.
19	Smoking, Drinking and consuming intoxicants are strictly prohibited.
20	Cold, stale, dry & spicy food should be avoided.
21	Sincere practice of first kriya can endow a practitioner with all siddhis & self-realization.
22	By regular practice of Kriya, longevity of the practitioner increases. There is also increase in the duration of Samadhi.
23	This world gets manifested as a result of the work of three gunas (Sata, Raja and Tama). Ida vein represents Tamoguna, the Pingla-Raja and the Sushumna represents the Satoguna.

24	Kutastha is the Sadguru. So, the result of kriya-practice should be sacrificed at the altar of the Kutastha.
25	Undivided devotion (single focused devotion) is necessary for success. It is the sine-qua-non for self- realization.
26	<u>The practice of original kriya shows instant result.</u>
27	The desire is at the root of (Samkalpa) a firm decision. If there is no desire , the mind will not be afraid of future. One desire gives birth to a series of desires and determinations.
28	Whatever you are doing, is the result of your past decisions and determinations.
29	The decisions and determinations of the past life surface automatically. It is called (Prarabdha) luck.
30	The common religious sacrifices (yagya) and fasting are included in it (Samkalpa).
31	Kriya practice is the true worship. It is the panacea for all ailments in this Iron Age.
32	Believe in the motto "There is only one truth" and "one without the other" (Ekmeva Advitiyam).
33	Doing a work for the sake of result is the cause of fulfilment of desires by using sense-organs (Vishaya – bhoga).
34	Guard yourself against unnecessary decisions and determinations.
35	Consider all the works to be the works of the God (Brahma).
36	You do not belong to any body nor does anybody belong to you. One must have this feeling- especially before performing the Kriya-practice.

37	Kriya-practice enables the sadhakas to recollect from memory information regarding previous incarnations.
38	One should not perform kriya-practice when it thunders or lightning takes place.
39	An important feature of a sadhaka is to perceive God (Narayana) in the beings (jeevas) and to harbor no discriminatory thought on the basis of caste, color, race etc.
40	Mind is our best friend if it is under control. If it is not under control, it is the worst enemy.
41	Kriya-practice is the true recital of the Vedas (Vedapatha).
42	With the improved 'Saman vayu' 'the Uttam Purush' is visible. (To be learnt from the Sadguru)
43	On performing the Kriya with prana vayu, the sadhka feels the taste of honey in the throat.
44	Advanced kriya-practitioners are the Brahmanas, those who remain absorbed in the Kriya-practice are the Kshatriyas, those who perform kriya-practice with worldly desires are the Vaishyas and those who do not practice kriya are the Shudras.
45	The sound of 'Om' is heard by the Brahmana (the best) sadhakas by practicing kriya for eleven days, for the Kshatriya (determined) sadhakas it is thirteen days, for the Vaishya (mediocre) sadhakas this time span is for sixteen days and it is thirty one days for the Shudra (the worst) sadhakas. At this time itself, the eternal star (Nakshatra) is visible in subtle form in the Kutastha. (to be learnt from the Sadguru).
46	Kriya-practice is the only means of self-realization in this Iron Age.

47	The sound of 'Om' listened to by the sadhakas during kriya-practice leads to increase in age and duration of samadhi to the Brahmin, it augments vigour to the kshatriya, it fills the Vaishya with hopes and desires and it fills the Shudra with hate.
48	The 'Kutastha' is present in all persons. Shri Babaji Maharaj Himself inspects the Kriya-practitioners in their 'Kutastha'.
49	'I' (the Atmaram) am always ready to ensure your spiritual progress.
50	On regular kriya-practice with utmost devotion for 1 to 3 years, a kriya-practitioner experiences a blissful state of intoxication and his head seems to be heavier. That is the first feature of the experience of Brahma.
51	The one who carries the load will get rid of it . You, the disciple, just keep on performing your duties (Kriya-practice).
52	Slow & steady wins the race. ("Banata-banata bani jayee, Hari se lage raho re Bhayee").
53	Regular practice for eight years gives consciousness (Divyagyan).
54	It is necessary to perform regular kriya –practice for 16 or 22 or 24 years. It is necessary to understand the kriya properly from the initiator. (Rev. Gurudeva) .
55	With continued kriya-practice ,the sadhaka experiences white colour in the head. It is due to the breathing through the three veins (Ida, Pingla & Sushumna) that one experiences black colour or the colour of smoke in the head.
56	Always worship the prana-brahma.
57	Do not criticize a good person.

58	As a result of regular kriya practice , there is increase in vigour as well as longevity. It leads the practitioner from darkness to light .
59	Do not use intoxicants.
60	Keep yourself tension-free during kriya-practice.
61	The Kriya-literature is the best for studies .
62	Do not try to get rid of your duties as a house-holder. Try to get rid of your ego i.e. 'I, My & Mine' Freeing oneself from ego is the real salvation.
63	Putting on saffron-robe & changing name do not make one a sanyasi. Remaining engaged in worldly affairs in a detached manner is the real sanyas.
64	The path of a house-holder is the best for the Kriya-practice .
65	To be a married person and to maintain a family is the foundation stone for self-realization. The unmarried people are prone to corrupt practices.
66	<u>Marriage is necessary for a kriya-practitioner.</u> It helps to experience the Nature & the Brahma.
67	Have devotion for the Guru who is none other than your own soul. A seeker in the beginning cannot feel this Guru . The Guru comes into experience in due course of the Kriya-practice with devotion.
68	Those who leave their houses are fickle-minded .They are restless people having unstable mind due to burning ambition. Such people cannot show the path to stability. The real Guru is self-absorbed, blissful, submerged in tranquility (Brahmamaya). Such Gurus appear before a seeker when his past good deeds start bearing fruits.

69	A seeker does not force himself into the garb of a sanyasi. Sanyas is a state of mind. A seeker automatically becomes a sanyasi after purity of mind as a result of regular Kriya-practice. Such a state of mind is the real sanyas.
70	True yogis appear like common people . Generally the common people cannot recognize them since they tend to hide themselves. They manifest themselves at appropriate times before the deserving seekers.
71	As a result of continued practice of pranayama, the Anahata Chakra gets pressurized which compels the mind to be one with the Brahma.
72	When a sadhaka has an experience of sweet liquid in the throat as a result of Pranavayu, he should **Swallow** it as if it were nectar.
73	Perform mantra–japa (meaning to be learnt from Rev. Gurudeva) with utmost devotion while performing kriya practice. Later on, this "japa" will be automatic and the Om can be heard.
74	When the 'Pranavayu' ascends upto the head, the best quality of Pranayama (Uttam Pranayama) is possible. So, continue with regular practice of pranayama with utmost devotion.
75	Practice of pranayama by putting maximum effort, ensures improved pranayama.
76	The way out of worldly pains is to remain detached from the worldly chores even while performing them. Whatever is destined to happen, is sure to take place.
77	The wealth is not a means to happiness. Why should we bother for the accumulation of unnecessary wealth? Why should we be concerned with future? Everybody in this world is like a dancing toy, the string of which is under the control of the God. People are tensed up because of their worldly pursuits – an outcome of stark ignorance.

78	Many Kriya-practitioners are incapable of performing the japa on the chakras. It transforms their Kriya-practice into the Tamasik state and the result is also like-wise. **It is, therefore, essential to perform 'Omkar-japa' on all the six chakras.**
79	At the time of performing 'Omkar–Kriya', the **japa must be performed on all the six chakras.** Sitting for the Kriya-practice , performing pranayama and keeping the mind on worldly desires lead the seekers nowhere. Such a practice becomes just normal breathing because the brain keeps on thinking about the worldly things, matters, people, situations etc.
80	Do not practice Kriya when you feel like sleeping.
81	Try to be awake at around 4 a.m.(Brahmavela)This time is appropriate for the Kriya-practice.
82	The Kriya –practice is not an ordinary practice. It requires whole-hearted efforts on a continuous basis for years.
83	Pranayama is the essence of all the Kriyas.
84	Keep on performing the Kriya-practice regularly while discharging your worldly duties.
85	Inhaling and exhaling are the feet of the God .Have a firm grip on these feet i.e. Keep on performing the japa while inhaling or exhaling.
86	The obsession with God-realisation leads to appearance of the Sadguru before a seeker.
87	Practicing 1000 kriya in a month removes all the sins of a practitioner.
88	Seeing the Kutastha in the body also helps to get rid of sins of practitioners.

89	Kutastha itself is the God.
90	Pranayama itself is tapa.
91	Religion is the real friend of human –beings.
92	Non-violence is the essence of religion.
93	Pleasure lies in the state of mind, not with wealth and other worldly things .
94	Greed is the worst enemy. So a greedy person is never peaceful.
95	If one is freed from greed , properties & wealth belonging to others seem to be worthless for a seeker.
96	Everything that belongs to 'I, Me or Mine' should be bestowed upon the Guru's feet.
97	No work is more important than the inner journey of mind.
98	Keep on performing kriya with devotion, you will come to know everything.
99	Do not insult or put to loss anybody without a reason.
100	Be kind to all creatures.
101	Do not be annoyed with an angry man.
102	Take the food which can enhance the 'Satoguna'.
103	Do not argue without knowing the subject-matter .
104	Try to inculcate the feeling of a Sadhu.
105	Give courage to the afraid people.
106	Do not sleep on a soft bed.

107	Be peaceful and patient.
108	Try to tolerate criticism and hash words from others.
109	Always try to provide food, clothes, shelter etc. to the needy to the extent possible.
110	Be polite and develop an ideal character.
111	Thinking of others (men or women) is a sin.
112	Do not harbour animosity towards anybody . The wavering mind itself is the real enemy.
113	Treat other ladies with motherly affection.
114	Do not try to peep into others' affairs. It spreads all types of vices (Prapancha).
115	Regularly perform the Kriya-practice twice a day reposing unconditional faith on utterances of Rev.Gurudeva.
116	Keep clean the points of outlets of secretions (urine, stool, sweat, etc.) i.e. body cleanliness.
117	Forgiving, kindliness and equanimity are the important features of a Kriya-practitioner.
118	Do not perform the Kriya-practice when it thunders or there is a cyclone or when you are tired.
119	Do not allow the ego to raise its ugly head as a result of supernatural experiences gained from the Kriya-practice.
120	Treat all advanced Kriya-practitioners as Rev.Gurudeva.

121	Those who have been able to revert their tongue and stretch it up to the hollow (the point where throat and nose meet) are Rev. Gurudevas in human form since they remain self-absorbed.
122	Ostentations of wealth , magical oratory , gimmicks and worldly powers (the aishwarya) have nothing to do with the features of Rev. Sadguru.
123	Being in the company of a realized person provides peace and pleasure.
124	The open discussion regarding the Kriya –practice and the experiences gained in through it should be confined only to the initiator.
125	Kriya-practice itself bestows upon the practitioner all types of siddhis (spiritual prowess).
126	Remain in the hot pursuit of kriya, not the siddha kriya-practitioner since he also has attained to this state by dint of kriya-practice.
127	Only those who have realized 'Brahma' during 'Samadhi'-state; are the Brahmins.
128	The mind is like a horse which can be reined in by nothing but the Kriya-practice.
129	Only a Kriya-practitioner (tapaswi) can keep in control the eleven elements like five work organs (hands, feet, mouth, penis & rectum.) five sense organs (eyes, nose, ears, tongue & skin) and the mind.
130	Devoid of the longings for touch, sight & taste etc.—— the ever content person is called jitendriya (the one who has conquered sense-organs & work-organs) (indriyas).

131	The 'Chaitanya samadhi' symbolizes the state of being one with the Brahma (Brahmaleena). In such a situation, the mind keeps on moving up and down on the six chakras.
132	Talk less. Do not talk without being asked. Engage yourself less and less in worldly gossips.
133	Regular kriya-practice makes the practitioners inquisitive & helps in tranquilizing or fixating the intellect. (buddhi).
134	Propagating about oneself that one is a good kriya-practitioner, is strictly prohibited since it makes the practitioner more egoistic. Always remember that the Rev.Gurudev is using you as an instrument for kriya-practice.
135	Perform kriya-practice with no desires.
136	The 'void' can be encountered only in the 'Sushumna'. 'Dhyana' will be stable only when the practitioner enters the Sushumna.
137	After ten years of regular Kriya-practice, the practitioner feels his body to be an embodiment of 'Omkar'.
138	Out of father & initiator, the initiator (Rev.Gurudev) is superior because it is the initiator who paves the way to self-realization (Brahma-Gyan).
139	Neither the old are great, nor the young ordinary. If a young person is self-realised, he needs to be venerated. It is what our scriptures command (Devavani).
140	The saints do not express their anguish, (pain). They do not hurt others.
141	The saintly people hide their spiritual prowess.
142	Always sleep alone in bed.

143	Avoid wasting semen & —————
144	The desire for sexual intercourse saps the enthusiasm for kriya-practice . So avoid sexual desires.
145	Silent Kriya is advisable to the pregnant ladies. Pranayama is not allowed during this period .
146	Keep on practicing kriya whether Rev. Guru says so or not.
147	**Wrong practice of the Kriya is of no use.**
148	The effective outcome in the form of attainment of peace and over-all welfare can be had only when the Kriya-practitioner performs the Kriya-practice precisely following the guidelines provided by Rev. Gurudeva.
149	Higher kriya-practitioners can ensure fixation of prana between 'Vishuddhaksha' and 'Agyan' chakras.
150	The 'Uttam Purush' can be seen only when the mind & intellect enter the Sushumna.
151	Perform kriya-practice regularly. You, too will be able to let your mind and intellect enter the Sushumna.
152	No outside material is required for kriya-practice. Only the prana is used for its practice.
153	Do not talk while lying in bed.
154	Answer a question only when you are asked.
155	Do not talk while eating.
156	Keep away from those who criticize Rev.Gurudeva or the kriya (Atmakarma).

157	Be seated on a seat lower than that of Rev.Guru.
158	Rev. Gurudeva's guru is none but Venerated Gurudeva.
159	Higher kriya practitioners should be considered to be like Rev.Gurudeva.
160	Those who have seen the 'Kutastha-bindu' by dint of Kriya-practice & have heard 'Anahat sound' are none but Rev. Gurudeva in human form. Be in their company .
161	Perform devoted Kriya practice in the morning & in the evening.
162	The whole world is replete with 'the void' i.e. Brahma for a sadhaka. So respect everybody from your inner core of heart.
163	Put maximum effort to Kriya-practice. As you experience the outcome, so will you increase the momentum of Kriya-practice.
164	Devotion to Muladhara, the dhyana of the Kutastha and the experience of Brahma are real religious practices(prakrit Dharma).
165	Those who keep on performing Kriya-practice throughout their lives, become one with the Brahma without fail.
166	An uncalled visitor should be considered to be the guest. Try to satisfy the God in the guest by providing food, water & seat with respect.
167	The real guest stays for one or two nights only.
168	When people are surrounded by problems , they call the God. The atheist also implore the God when they are neck-deep in problems. Keep on doing the work assigned to you.

169	Desire for worldly pleasures is at the root of misery and discontentment with pain.
170	Do not be disheartened if you do not have supernatural experiences from the Kriya-practice. Continue with the Kriya-practice ensuring japa on all the Chakras ,you will eventually succeed one day or the other. Remember — —<u>we may be dishonest but the Rev. Gurudeva and the Kriya can never be dishonest .</u>
171	Always meditate upon the Guru (soul or the Kutastha).
172	Always focus on your breathing .
173	If the attachment to worldly affairs get completely transferred to the Kriya-practice, the practitioner can quickly arrive at his or her destination.
174	Rev. Babaji Maharaj keeps on observing the Kriya-practitioners all the time but we miserably fail to keep our attention on Him i.e. the Kriya-practice. People are generally drawn to worldly activities with deep-rooted attachments. The devoted Kriya-practitioners do get a glimpse of Rev. Babaji Maharaja.
175	Keep on practicing the Kriya with patience and perseverance . All the hindrances will automatically be removed just by the virtue of your devotion and tenacity.
176	Regulation of prana is the only Sattwic karma .
177	Keep on practicing the Kriya to the best of your ability and capacity. Whoever is called by a devoted Kriya-practitioner, visits him or her without fail .
178	The Kriya-yoga is not merely a technique .Its devoted practice leads to the attainment of the state beyond gunas. Later on, it leads to liberation.

179	**Omkar-kriya must be practiced every day.**
180	Atmakarma or the Kriya-yoga is the real worship.
181	The bondage caused by the illusion(Maya) is subtle. It is extremely difficult to transcend it. It is possible only with the benediction from Rev. Gurudeva.(Guru-kripa).
182	The main function of mind is to keep on pondering on various alternatives (Sankalpa/vikalpa) i.e. thinking for initiating an action or non-action in future. Keep on practicing the Kriya in order to purify this mind (manas).
183	Without arousing the inner thirst, longings for worldly things do not cease. The Kriya-practice promotes the growth of this inner thirst.
184	A desire cannot overcome other desires. Only the Kriya-practice can bestow upon a seeker desire-less state. A seeker gets rid of the epidemic of unceasing desires only on the attainment of the desireless state.
185	A Kriya-practitioner effortlessly attains supernatural prowess.
186	Anybody can be a kriya-practitioner. It is the true path for the attainment of peace in this Iron age.
187	Consider yourself to be an agent of the God (soul/Guru). It is the only escape route from the tyranny of ego. Everybody should always keep this fact in mind. "निमित्तमात्रं भव सव्यसाचिन्" ("Nimittamatram bhava savyasachi".)
188	Do not fall a prey to Astrology or palmistry. Keep on performing your duties. God Himself takes care of you.
189	As "Chiraita-water" is a remedy for "pitta-problem", the "Kriya-practice" in the same way is the panacea for mental ailments.

190	For the success in kriya-practice, japa on chakras is a must.
191	Atma / soul is the real Guru .So keep your focus of attention on the soul.
192	Ensure that regular inspection of kriya-practice is done by your guide, who has taught you the 'kriya-techniques'.
193	Do not make false promises. Do not talk if not required. Speak less i.e. only when required. The first-kriya will provide you with seriousness and you will have the desire to talk less.
194	This world keeps on changing according to its inherent nature. Do your own work and let the events take their own course.
195	Kriya-practice with devotion is the panacea for all type of suffering.
196	Always keep your focus of attention on the Kutastha.
197	Consider the person to be your guide in whose company you are filled with an intense desire for the Kriya-practice.
198	Be aloof from worldly desires since the Kriya- practice with worldly desires will bear no positive outcome.
199	All the three knots (Muladhara, Anahata & Agyan) are pierced in the Sushumna.
200	The wavering tendency of mind is but natural. In order to stop this wavering tendency of mind practice of the Kriya-yoga is required.
201	One is face to face with the Sadguru only when one is obsessed for the God.
202	Service to Rev. Gurudeva i.e. kriya-practice is the duty above all.
203	This duty is our natural friend also.

204	With increase in the Kriya- practice the emotion of jealousy ceases to exit.
205	Try to keep the place & blanket used for the Kriya-practice extremely personal & maintain regularity in respect of the Kriya-practice.
206	On practicing Kriya for three hours each day, the practitioner is endowed with all the spiritual powers .
207	Try your level best to keep your mind free from worldly thoughts.
208	Be alert the moment longing for worldly things try to captivate your mind.
209	If the mind continues to wander in the jungle of this world even during kriya-practice (it yields no result) it goes in vain.
210	The garb of a sadhu leads to crimes of different types.
211	Try to make yourself the real saint from the core of your heart.
212	It is useless to perform kriya-practice in order to get respect and adoration from others.
213	Collective exhibition of the Kriya-practice is prohibited. The Kriya-practice should not be performed before non-kriya practitioners.
214	Avoid direct or indirect publicity of your name since it causes a great hindrance to the Kriya- practice .
215	A Kriya-practitioner should be resolute in approach, moderate in behaviour and brimful of patience.
216	Perform the Kriya –practice with firm determination. It must be remembered that the Rev. Sadguru supervises all the sincere practitioners.

217	When the sadhaka is emotionally resolute, the Rev. Sadguru manifests before him.
218	On continuing with correct Kriya-practice , the spiritual prowess of all types are easily available.
219	Make a regular perusal of Rev. Yogiraj's commentaries on the 'Gurugita' and 'Shrimad Bhagwad Gita'. Follow the instructions given therein without even a shred of doubt.
220	The Kriya-practice with worldly desires is strictly prohibited . Hence avoid worldly desires.
221	Practice 'Yonimudra' (Darshan) after completing all the kriyas. It will stabilize the energy produced in course of the Kriya- practice and the practitioner is able to listen the sound of Om and see the divine light (Jyoti).
222	Do not give importance to this outer world. Be indifferent to the comments passed by people and concentrate on the Kriya practice.
223	Whatever you get as a result of your work (labour), be content with that.
224	Protest against injustice if necessary but it must be in keeping with time & situation.
225	It is better not to meet people who criticize the Kriya.
226	Maintain a safe distance while talking to non-kriya practitioners.
227	When there is secretion of nectar from the head of a 'kriya-practitioner, he will attain tranquility or stability of mind and the body will also be healthy.

228	In this human body itself, there is " कल्पवृक्ष:" 'Kalpabriksha'. You can see it when the mind gets tranquilized or stabilized.
229	All the desires get automatically fulfilled if a kriya-practitioner performs Kriya-practice with devotion.
230	Do not abuse your body in worldly pleasures.
231	The world is ever changing. Hence, do not get attached to it. Perform your duties as if they were assigned to you by the God.
232	Do not eat too much at a time.
233	Do not eat at dawn and dusk.
234	If by any reason you have taken a little more food during day time, do not eat at night or eat just a little bit at night.
235	Do not speak loudly.
236	Do not talk much since there is possibility of lying when you talk much.
237	Running fast, jumping, dancing vigorously etc. are prohibited.
238	Sit for the Kriya-practice after attending the call of nature.
239	Kriya-practice at night or around 4 a.m. is advisable.
240	Do not eat stale or cold food nor should you drink polluted water.
241	Do not eat at an unknown place or with unknown person.
242	Try to be vegetarian so far as possible.
243	Those who have had the experience of the Kutastha, are wise and one with the Brahma.

244	Even the destiny cannot harm them who keep on performing kriya.
245	Kriya-practice is not allowed at a place where the wind is blowing hard.
246	Do not perform kriya-practice during hurricanes, typhoon or storm.
247	Do not practice kriya if it thunders or there is lightning.
248	Do not practice kriya in case of burning of a star or the meteors (GukeÀeHeele).
249	There is no restriction on kriya-practice if there is a birth or death in the family since there is nothing impious for kriya-practice.
250	Perform the Kriya-practice with the precise japa of 'Om'.
251	Do not perform kriya-practice if you are ill.
252	Do not be hostile to any one without a reason.
253	Those who practice kriya correctly, are always blessed with all-round success.
254	The Kriya-practice is the real worship, the rest are (subsidiary) an aid to it.
255	Kriya-practice leads to formation of sound character.
256	Those who do not practice Kriya, remain restless and diseased.
257	The Kriya-practice with worldly desires leads to grief.
258	Do not be jealous of anyone.
259	Keep your tongue & other organs under control.

260	The destiny becomes slave of those who remain in 'void'.
261	Do not donate to the wicked and those who don the guise of a saint but are crooked indeed. They should not even be touched.
262	Do not trust those who try to prove themselves to be saint on the strength of oratory.
263	People having outer features of a hermit (eg. Long beard, long hairs, saffron robe, sacred symbol on the forehead) should not be relied upon.
264	The real saints appear to be ordinary in this world itself and, therefore, it is extremely difficult to identify them.
265	They will manifest themselves before you when you are obsessed with the desire for enlightenment.
266	They do not accept any worldly gift without a reason.
267	They follow the rules of nature.
268	They lead the life of a householder. (Rev. Yogiraj is himself an example.)
269	Do not take anything from anybody without his permission.
270	Do more and more practice of 'First-Kriya'. Try to keep your tongue inverted in order to get away from the torture of worldly attachments.
271	Keep on increasing the kriya-practice gradually.
272	Do not eat non-vegetarian food just for bodily force or taste.
273	Anything can be eaten with any one for mere survival (in case of famine).

274	**Sexual relationship with anyone other than husband/wife is strictly prohibited.**
275	Engage yourself in ideal coitus just for having a child.
276	Sexual intercourse should not be viewed to be something which gives pleasure.
277	Do not betray your husband/wife.
278	Restrain your sense-organs as well as work-organs.
279	Do not look down upon anyone.
280	Social behavior should be guided by (Varna and karma)..............
281	It is useless to follow caste-system at present since the present caste-system does not conform to 'class-division' JeCe & - J³eJemLee.
282	Following useless practices or norms leads to mental disturbance and jealousy.
283	Always drink filtered water.
284	Speak the truth but avoid unpleasant and bitter truth.
285	There must be complete conformity between your thoughts & deeds.
286	Do not be angry on an annoyed person.
287	Lust, anger, greed and attachment - these are the four main hindrances to the Kriya-practice for a Kriya-practitioner.
288	Mental peace is attained by the Kriya-practice & not by oratory skills.

289	If you have committed unintentional mistake which has harmed someone, you should perform six pranayamas by way of a token of repentance.
290	Gold glitters after coming out of fire. In the same way, the mind and body improve dramatically as a result of pranayama.
291	The world cannot enslave the one who is one with the Brahma since he remains detached even if he performs all his worldly duties.
292	Kriya-practice puts an end to diseases, sorrow and pain.
293	1728 pranayamas lead to ultimate accomplishments.
294	Leading the life of a householder is the best for the Kriya-practice.
295	A Kriya-practitioner is greater than many worldly achievers.
296	Kriya-practice leads to God-realization / self-realization.
297	Try to view the world as a witness or a detached person (indifferent onlooker).
298	12 Pranayamas – pratyahar, 144 pranayamas-dharana, 1728 pranayamas - dhyana & 20736 pranayamas - samadhi.
299	Do not practice Kriya when you feel sleepy.
300	Do not practice pranayama when you are yawning.
301	Do not practice Kriya before a non-kriya-Practitioner.
302	Do not divulge the techniques of Kriya to anyone.
303	Kriya-practice is the best when done in privacy (alone).

304	Continual Kriya-practice before Rev. Gurudeva is necessary.
305	Get your Kriya-practice checked from time to time.
306	One must get his Kriya-practice checked within two weeks after being initiated & again within three months, from this date.
307	Later on, a practitioner must get his Kriya-practice checked once in a year.
308	Proper Kriya-practice makes the practitioner intoxicated. It indicates that Kriya-practice is being done properly. This intoxication keeps on increasing - leading to the state of paravastha (tranquil state).
309	Nabhi Kriya (to be learnt from Rev. Gurudeva) leads to stabilization of mind and samana vayu (….) and it brings about refinement in pranayama.
310	Mahamudra (to be learnt from Rev. Gurudeva) increases the aura and vigor of the body.
311	Whenever you get time and you feel like practicing Kriya, sit for the Kriya-practice.
312	The Kriya –practice should be increased during winter.
313	The Kriya-practice should be undertaken three hours after lunch or heavy meal.
314	No cold drink (any liquid including water) should be had just after the Kriya practice.
315	Any solid food can be eaten half an hour after the Kriya-practice.
316	Taking bath just after the Kriya practice is prohibited.

317	Walking just after the Kriya practice is prohibited. Remain seated for some time.
318	Six hours sleep is required.
319	A new Kriya-practitioner should be particular regarding regularity, time and place for the Kriya- practice.
320	If you keep on practicing the Kriya for ten years (to be understood from Rev. Gurudeva) strictly following the instructions of Rev. Gurudeva, you are sure to have the self-realization.
321	You must discharge your responsibilities for parents, wife/husband & children. It will help in the Kriya-practice.
322	Discharge your worldly responsibilities considering them to be Nature's work and the Kriya-practice should be deemed to be the Lord's work.
323	There is a difference between responsibility & attachment.
324	God dwells in all hearts. Respect everybody keeping in view this motto.
325	Keep the focus of your attention on the soul and not on the body.
326	So long as you are not able to have self-realisation, this world also will not appear to be replete with the Brahma everywhere.
327	Pranavayu is nothing but the God (Paramatma) .There is nothing greater than this which can provide you the shelter .
328	Rev. Gurudeva knows everything . Do not ask for any worldly thing from Him.
329	Have the only expectation of 'self-realization' from Rev. Gurudeva. He is capable enough to provide it to you.

330	Rev. Gurudeva is present in your 'Kutastha'. It is useless to search Him outside.
331	It is sheer waste of precious life to engage oneself in outer form of worship when one has been initiated into the Kriya-yoga.
332	The previous sanskaras have an effect on the Kriya-practice.
333	The ultimate duty of a human being is to know himself in the real sense.
334	Good and bad choices are always before you.
335	You do not have to imagine the Kutastha. It manifests itself automatically.
336	Most of the people do not follow the instructions of Rev. Gurudeva. That is why they are sad.
337	If you do not derive pleasure out of the Kriya-practice, your intellect & mind are to be blamed for it. Go to your initiator and find a way out.
338	Performing a lot of kriya together is sheer waste of time.
339	The original Kriya-yoga is rare and different from those popular & easily available in the market in the name of Kriya.
340	Be frugal or economical , otherwise you will have to face scarcity.
341	Do not waste your (wealth) money.
342	Spend according to your income. Save yourself from ostentation.
343	Pranayama should be practiced slowly, with devotion & with mantra.

344	The internal pranayamas in the Kriya-yoga should not be practiced in haste.
345	Those who have useless desires are 'Chamar' (sudra).
346	Those who are desireless are Brahmins.
347	Do not engage yourself in debate on religion.
348	Try to get rid of 'laziness'.
349	It is not advised to sleep more than required. Sleeping causes laziness.
350	Spiritual discussions should be done by focusing on the Kutastha.
351	There are many obstacles for a Kriya-practitioner. Be patient & have devotion while continuing with the Kriya-practice. Everything will be okay.
352	There are disturbances in respect of time , place and even the Kriya-practice but you must have unwavering faith in Rev. Gurudeva.
353	The obstacles of the Kriya-practice can be removed by none but Rev.Gurudeva.
354	If you are extremely devoted to the Kriya-practice, all the hindrances get removed automatically.
355	The mind of a Kriya-practitioner tries to deceive him. Hence be extremely alert.
356	The knowledge derived by reading books or listening to people are dry and just not suitable for 'Vairagya' i.e renunciation / detachment.

357	Nothing but the Kriya practice can ensure attainment of the state of detachment.
358	The Kriya practice can enable you to know your past lives.
359	The Kriya-practice must be performed at the interval of twelve hours.
360	Pranayama (to be learnt from Rev. Gurudeva) is the essence of the Kriya-practice.
361	Have complete faith in the matters which are in complete conformity with the religious treatises.
362	It is a sin to criticize the Kriya .
363	**We may be dishonest but the Kriya cannot be so.**
364	Do not ignore your worldly duties. Not only the ordinary people but also the siddhas have to perform their worldly duties .
365	While performing worldly chores, keep in mind what is in your interest and what is not in your interest.
366	The past cannot be retrieved . Who knows the future?
367	The present belongs to you. Make its proper use since the future springs out of the womb of the present itself.
368	I (the Atmaram Guru) am always there in the Kutastha. See me there only.
369	The secret of success in the Kriya-practice lie in devotion & unwavering dedication to the Kriya- practice. It will pave the way to self-realization.

| 370 | On confessing the sins (theft, injustice, illicit relationships etc.) before Rev. Gurudeva , He destroys them by the Kriya practice. |
| 371 | The essence of a flower (smell) and the soul of a human being are subtle. Keep your focus on the subtle in order to be away from the 'Gross outer form'. |

**Photo : Books kept at Lahiri Baba's Room but now with
Aryya Mission at Kolkata.**

108 WORDS of WISDOM from Yogiraj Shri Shri LAHIRI MAHASAYA's Personal Diary

1	Kriya is Truth, and the rest is false.
2	Practicing Kriya is the study of the Vedas. Kriya is jagya (Yagya) [performance of Vedic rituals]. All should perform this jagya.
3	All Devatas, gods, practice these Kriyas. One who practices Kriya is a Devata.
4	One should practice Pranayama very seriously and sincerely.
5	Kriya practice opens the Eye of Wisdom.
6	The Knowledge of Brahma, the ultimate Self, is attained by the practice of Pranayama.
7	Ignorance is removed automatically when the Kriya practice is perfect.
8	By the practice of Pranayama, ignorance is dispelled and Knowledge of the Self reveals.
9	One who does not see Kutastha [the inner Self between the eyebrows] with the help of Guru's advice in this physical body is a blind person.
10	That which saves one from the mind [restless breath], or manasa, is called Mantra; that which saves one from the attachment of body is called Tantra.

11	The transcendence of inhaling and exhaling is called Kebala Kumbhaka.
12	**The practice of Khechari mudra brings victory over the senses.**
13	**When the tongue is raised, the senses are subdued.**
14	**If one attains the stabilized state in Khechari mudra, then he attains the state of Samadhi.**
15	**One whose Khechari is successful is fortunate.**
16	OM is radiant Light. When this Light is spread throughout the body, all is seen; then, there is no desire to speak and to look.
17	Air [Breath] is Lord.
18	When one continues to refine brown sugar, finally it becomes white. Similarly, continued Kriya practice brings Pranayama to perfection.
19	If one moves the breath [practices Pranayama] always, breath ceases and becomes tranquil, sthira.
20	The state of Sthirattva, Tranquility, is called Yoga.
21	Practice Kriya as long as possible sitting in one asana at least once a day.
22	If one strikes the door with the reverse air then it will open. This is called reverse japam. -

	- (That is, tranquilizing apana, the restless breath of the lower centers, and bringing up at the dorsal center and then if one strikes (makes thokar) according to the advice, then the inner Door will open).
23	Having practiced Kriya, one should hold onto the After-effect-poise of Kriya.
24	You will receive results according to your Kriya practice.
25	If you feel pain [during the Kriya practice] in the body, then understand that the practice is not going well.
26	The real work is to tune to meditation in Voidness [on the fifth element, ether] leaving three nerves: ida, pingala, susumna and four elements: khiti. apa, teja, and marut, respectively, earth, water, fire, and air.
27	When the mind is tranquil, it does not desire unnecessarily. At the state of beyond desire, one does not perform unnecessary works.
28	When one has attained the tranquil Breath, then, for him, the only work which remains is to hold onto the state of tranquility always.
29	It is difficult to express the state when the breath becomes tranquil, Sthira.
30	When the breath is tranquil day and night, then, one realizes the real state of Rama Mantra.

31	When the breath is tranquil, it is the state of Kumbhaka. When one sees Oneself, it is called Brahmajnana, "the Knowledge of Brahma, the ultimate Self."
32	There is no need to breath in or out. It is a much happier state; tranquility is there; this is Brahma.
33	One becomes Brahma when one becomes desireless
34	[Lahiri Mahasay's meditative life with Kriya was from 1861 to 1873. The following dates are found in his notebook:- **May 13, 1873** - Whatever one wants to do, he can do.
35	**June 29, 1873** - I entered inside [the Spinal Cord] a little bit.
36	**July 16, 1873** - The senses disturb today. I must renounce all desires and dissolve myself.
37	The senses are obstructions; Transcending them by the practice of Praanam and Omkar Kriyas, today, I have to dissolve perfectly. This is the only work for me.
38	It does not matter, if life departs from the physical body. I must practice Kriya with all my heart.
39	Kriya practice brings divine wealth, that is, Sthirattva, the state of Tranquility.
40	**Aug 13, 1873** - Now, always remain in Kumbhaka. This is the form of Mahadeva, Lord Siva; head was always heavy, the eyes were drawn above; this state does not break when inhaling is done; at that time, silence is very beneficial.

41	One can see all the deities if one withdraws the restless mind and makes inward himself in the Kutastha.
42	I saw Radhaji [consort of Krishna] at the base of the inner Sound.
43	The sun is Kali (Goddess Kali), I myself am Kali. Thinking about Kali I become Kali. Now I will be father of Kali, Brahma, the ultimate Self.
44	The sun is Kali [Goddess Kali], and I am what I am.
45	**Aug 13, 1873** - Today, I became Mahapurusa, "the great man."
46	**Aug 17, 1873** - I am Mahapurusa. In the sun I saw that I myself am Brahma, the ultimate Self.
47	**Aug 18, 1873** - The world is revealed from my form. I myself am the only Purusa, the supreme Being.
48	**Aug 18, 1873** - The world is revealed from my form. I myself am the only Purusa, the Self; there is nobody else.
49	**Aug 22, 1873** - I myself am Adi Purusa Bhagavan, the first Lord.
50	**Aug 23, 1873** - Whatever I say is Veda. Know it for certain.
51	**I saw four Vedas, Brahma, Visnu, and Maheswar (Lord Siva) inside the Yoni [between the eyebrows].**

52	I saw a blue color in the light; in the blue, I saw a white Spot (Bindu); and in the white Spot, I saw a man who manifested himself as a Hindu, English man, etc.
53	I saw thousands of Krishna's.
54	I saw the greater Krishna.
55	**Aug 24, 1873 - I myself am Lord Krishna.**
56	Aug 25, 1873 - I myself am the Aksara Purusa, the eternal Being. [It may be mentioned here that each rhythm of Consciousness of the seeker in the process of merging with the ultimate Self is a state of deity, or devata till he merges completely in Oneness with Brahma.]
57	**Oct 3, 1873** - I am the sun, the Mahadeva, the first cause.
58	**Nov 12, 1873** - I myself am Mahapurusa Purusottam, "the great Self, the supreme Being."
59	Aug 15, 1874 - It is not possible to achieve Abhaya pada, "the state of fearlessness" without the help of Guru. One must hold onto Oneself at the house of Tranquility, without which, one cannot achieve the Abhaya pada, the eternal Realization of the ultimate Self.
60	My form is everywhere; there is nobody except me, and that form is in Void. There is no day and night there.
61	If you take shelter in me with true faith, then, I have to come to you. How can I stay far away?

62	I remain present near one who practices Kriya.
63	If you write in reverse order and see it in the mirror, it looks straight. Similarly, if you make reverse the breath of the body, then you will see Swarupa, the form of yourself.
64	Dualism is the root of all suffering.
65	Restless is manifestation, and Sthirattva, Tranquility, is Lord Siva.
66	You yourself do not know what will render you good.
67	If the strain is generated on the lips, throat, and teeth by the practice of Pranayama, then the knowledge is called Bhakti, or devotion.
68	Whatever one thinks at the time of death, accordingly one becomes that; likewise, if you become Satchitananda at the time of leaving the body, then, you become yourself, the ultimate Self.
69	Who is Kabir? He is sun, and he is Brahma, myself. [These names are found from his notebook].
70	**In Satyayuga Lahiri Mahasay was born as Satyasukrita, in tretayuga he was Munindra; in dwaparayuga Karunamaya; and in kaliyuga he was Kabir. Later, he became Shyama Charan.**
71	If one meditates always on the Lord, all his other works are taken care of by the Lord Himself.

72	If people want to go away, let them go away; but you should remain firm in your practice. Then, at the end, you will go into the house of Sthirattva, Tranquility.
73	The movement is called world.
74	Applying body, mind, and speech in action is called Ahingsa [Non- violence].
75	Animals are enchanted by music; if man is not attracted by the sound of OM, then he is an ass.
76	Beyond the five senses there is mind, that is breath; beyond the mind there is buddhi, that is bindu, or spot [in between the eyebrows]; beyond the bindu, Brahma, the ultimate Self, is the Pure Void, and Formless.
77	Woman is the destroyer of man. Do not look at her, at any cost. Note: [The sun of the self, that is, sound, is referred to here as man; and the jyoti, light of the self, is referred to as woman. In other words, do not be interested in the play of jyoti, or develop attachment to the inner visions; after all, visions are secondary and are not inner Realization. [It is sound, Om, or Nada, which helps the seeker to go beyond bindu and merge into Oneness with Brahma, the ultimate Self].
78	I saw a pure Void, that is Brahma, the ultimate Self. The mind must be dissolved in It.
79	Mind should not be made outward. What's the benefit if the mind and the eyes are tranquil and not the body? Today, the breath does not come out, and a lot of addictions are generated.

80	Merging in pure Voidness is called Samadhi.
81	Beyond Purusottam, the supreme Being, there is Brahma, the ultimate Self.
82	Without being niskama, that is, totally detached, there is no possibility to be merged in Brahma. [When the seer destroys his character as seer and becomes one with the ultimate Self, then dualism is dissolved].
83	Voidness which is inside voidness is called great Voidness, Brahma.
84	**Satyayuga is the After-effect-poise of Kriya; tretayuga is the temporary After-effect-poise of Kriya; dwaparayuga is to practice Kriya; and when one does not practice I, it is kaliyuga for him.**
85	When one transcends Basu, desires, he becomes Dev, the Lord; that is, he becomes Basudev, or Lord Krishna.
86	One becomes Basudev when the basanas, the desires, are transcended. He is the Lord.
87	A liar who cannot keep his word is not a good man; his father, that is, his Lord is also no good.
88	The essence of Rama-mantra is to place the tongue into Talabya Kriya and continue to listen the sound of Om.
89	Inside this body there is another body which is somewhat black.
90	Knowledge of the ultimate Self is to know Oneself by oneself.

91	Looking at the middle of the forehead, which is above the nose and eyebrows, is a bit difficult; if one stabilizes on this, he attains the state of Samadhi.
92	Till Bhishma [grandfather of Kaurava and Pandava], that is, fear [in the light of Kriya Bhisma means fear of practicing Kriya], receives three arrows, that is, ida, pingala and susumna in his head [unite in the Kutastha], never becomes Sthira, tranquil; One should practice Kriya courageously.
93	Nobody is a sinner; no one is holy either; if the mind is put into the Kutastha, then, there is no sin; otherwise, if the mind is outward, there is sin; in other words, when the mind is not in the Kutastha, it is in sin.
94	The old father (Babaji) is Lord Krishna.
95	I saw Saptarsi, seven Yogis (Bhrigu, Atri, Angira, Marichi, Pulastya, Pulaha, and Kratu; and four Manus (Sanaka, Sananda, Sanatan, and Sanat Kumar].
96	All sins are destroyed at the After-effect-poise of Kriya.
97	Avidya, ignorance, is the outward state of mind; Bidya, Knowledge, is the After-effect-poise of Kriya.
98	One who practices Pranayama, truly loves all beings.
99	Slowly, slowly, all works are being done.
100	Worldly beautiful things are poisonous. If you see them outwardly, they attract you; but if you see them inwardly, then, they are renounced. This is maya, or restlessness.

101	Let others go as they please, but you continue to practice Kriya; It will render you good; You will achieve the state of Tranquility, Sthirattva.
102	One can say everything when the Kriya practice continues spontaneously at the six centers.
103	Nobody is a sinner; the mind itself is the sinner when it becomes outward away from the Kutastha.
104	Tranquil Moment beyond breath is Allah, that is, the House of Tranquility.
105	Brahma is Pure; It has not come out from anything; in other words, Brahma is ever Pure and Brahma is never tasted before by anyone. [Tasting something is possible from the state of dualism. But if one becomes one with Brahma, one becomes Brahma himself. So there is no possibility to taste Brahma. As a result, Brahma remains ever untasted, Pure].
106	Do not be idle. Practice Kriya. Do not wait for advice to practice Kriya.
107	Exhaust your breath in practicing Kriya. Eventually breath will be Sthira, Tranquil.
108	All realization is possible by the practice of the Kriya & Higher Kriyas. One is required to practice strictly according to the instructions received from one's Guru personally.

Letters between Guru (Yogiraj Rev.Shyamacharan Lahiri) and Disciple (Yogacharya Rev.Panchanan Bhattcharya)

Om

The correspondence between Rev.Yogiraj Shri Shyama Charan Lahiri and Rev.

Yogacharya Shri Panchanan Bhattacharya is being published for the first time.

(as per olddocuments of the Arya Mission Institution).

(originally in Bengali)

<h1 style="text-align:center"><u>Letter No.1</u></h1>

Priyanath Karar mahasaya (Later on known as Swami Yukteshwar Giri) has sent 10 copies of his Gita to me but people here do not want to buy this Gita. If you allow, people will accept it.

Prostrating before you

Your servant
Shri Panchanan Bhattacharya

Letter (Replied):

Ask the people to buy the Gita published by Prasaddas Goswami (Disciple of Lahiri Baba residing at Shri Rampur). Later on, those who are willing to buy the Gita of Priyanath, may buy. Very soon everything relating to Priyanath will be known to all.

Shri Shyama Charan Devasharman
12/3/1888

<u>Letter No.2</u>

To,
Tinkauri Lahiri (the eldest son of Lahiri Baba)
C/O Babu Panchanan Bhattacharya
Kolkata.

Convey that everything is okay here. There is simply nothing to worry about.

Shri Shyama Charan Devasharman
2/3/1885

<u>Letter No.3</u>

Salutation to Shri Durga (Shri Durga smarnam)

You have not yet sent the money received from initiating people. Hope that it will not happen soon. Inform Tinkauri that Kalicharan was not promoted. Whatever happened, is okay.

Shri Shyama Charan Devasharman
5/6/1885

<u>**Letter No. 4**</u>

(Salutations to Shri Durga)
Namaskar,

'I too am not under my own control'-this state has been clearly explained in the 'Markandeya Purana. Please write to me about the expenses involved in the publication of this book but the mystery of time explained in the book, which explains the method of finding out when a person isgoing to die, must not be published. The rest is okay.

Shri Shyama Charan devasharman
12/05/1890

<u>**Letter No.5**</u>

Namaskar,
(Salutation to Shri Durga)

Please send the details of expenses to be incurred in the publication of the following books: The Gita (i.e. Aryya Mission Gita of the size of Rs.2) 'Vaisheshika' 'Kabir' (part-2), 'Tantrasar', 'Markandeya Purana', 'Manu', 'Aushdhavali', 'Sankhya', 'Bhagawat Ekadesh skandh', 'Charak'.

Shri Shyama Charan Devasharman
Nov.1,1893

Letter No.6

Namaskar,

Received 50 copies of 'Tattariya Upanishad'. Please send this book to the Kriya practitioners who (contact you through letters) maintain correspondence with you. If possible, please send some more copies of this book. Shri Dayal Babu (a disciple of Shri Lahiri Baba) is going to see you. If possible, send some copies of the book through him.

Shri Shyama Charan Devasharman

Letter No.7

Shri Panchanan Babu,

Do not initiate a Sanyasi by robe or by name. They just give the outer manifestation of a Sanyasi. They are not able to control soon the outwardly longings of their heart. In my opinion, only the householders are eligible for initiation. Please send the news regarding Tinkauri.

Shri Shyama Charan Devasharman

<u>**Letter No.8**</u>

Om guruve namah

After Salutation -
Dukauri Bhai,

I have handed over the sum of money received from initiation to the supreme Guru Shri Babaji Maharaj. Accept my Namaskara. You yourself please hand over the sum of money received from initiation to Him.

Shri Panchanan Devasharman

<h2 style="text-align:center"><u>Letter No.9</u></h2>

Baba, (Yogiraj Shyamacharan Lahiri)

Me with family at your kind and divine feet,

     The Annapurna Puja was celebrated during the last two years here, at Kolkata. Everybody wants to celebrate it this year too but I am undecided. If you order, it will be celebrated, otherwise I do not intend to celebrate it since you are the Almighty for me. You do everything but people think that I do it. What should be done? In order to know, I am writing this letter to you.

The servant at your feet.
Shri Panchanan Bhattacharya

<u>**Letter No.10**</u>

Baba,
After Salutation to your divine feet,

The Arya Mission's works are being performed properly. If a kriya-practitioner from Varanasi can teach the Gita here in the school it will be of great help to us. As you know it very well, the Arya Mission Gita has already been published. The moment you permit, it will be distributed among people. Here so many people are committing mistakes in 'Nabhikriya' and 'Yonimudra' even now. Even now they do not have any significant experience. What should be done?

Your servant
Panchanan Bhattacharya

<u>**Letter Replied :**</u>

Shriman (Respected) Panchanan Babu,

The Guru is watching everything. In spite of teaching the Kriya people commit mistakes during Kriya-practice but they love to blame the Kriya-practice. The more the number of wrong sanskaras, the more will be wrong Kriya-practice. Such a practitioner will come to the right path after many lives (pranayamas).

At the time of initiation, a copy of the Gita can be given to the practitioners. Please send one hundred copy of the Gita here. It is advisable to ensure free distribution of this book. Now I do not intend to meet people any more. I am going to send more people to you for initiation. Initiate after careful examination. The rest is possible only after surrendering to the self. (Durga Sharanapanna).

Shri Shyama Charan Devasharman
26/6/1890

Guru kripa hi kewalam

(Only on blessings of Gurudev)

Shyama Charan Lahiri (30 September 1828 – 26 September 1895), best known as Lahiri Mahasaya, was an Indian yogi guru who founded the Kriya Yoga school. In 1861, his non-physical master Mahavatar Babaji appeared to him, ordering him to revive the yogic science of Kriya Yoga to the public after centuries of its guarding by masters. He was unusual among Indian holy people in that he was a householder, marrying, raising a family, and working as a government accountant, an "Ideal yogi-householder." He became known in the West through Paramahansa Yogananda, a disciple of Sri Yukteswar Giri, and through Yogananda's 1946 book *Autobiography of a Yogi*, considering him a *Yogavatar*, or "Incarnation of Yoga," since Lahiri himself was chosen by the yogic masters to disseminate the principles of yoga to the world.

Panchanan Bhattacharya (1853–1919) was a chief disciple of the Indian Yogi Lahiri Mahasaya. He was the first disciple to be authorized by Lahiri Mahasaya to initiate others into Kriya Yoga, and helped to spread Lahiri Mahasaya's teachings in Bengal through his Arya Mission Institution.

Shrimati Kashi Moni Devi—Wife of the Yogiraj
Sri Sri Lahiri Mahasaya

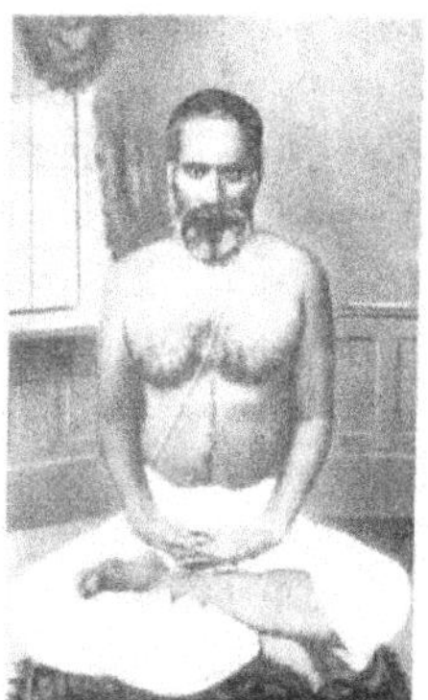

Shri Shri Tincouri Lahiri Mahasaya
(Eldest son of the Yogiraj on the Left)

Shri Shri Ducouri Lahiri Mahashaya
(Younger son of the Yogiraj on the Right)

Yogiguru Shrimat Brahmachari Anilanandaji Maharaj

Ramkrishnapur Brahmachary Anilananda Research Institute

Yogiswar Shriguru Matilal Thakur
Advent: 30 December, 1866 (15 Paus, 1273 B. S. AgrahayaniKrishnastami)
Mahasamadhi: 10 October, 1945 (23Ashwin,1352B.S.)

<u>Acharya Shri Matilal Thakur, first disciples of Shri Yukteshwar Giri</u>

Matilal Thakur was the foremost disciple of Shriyukteswar. He dedicated his life to his Guru and assisted him in every possible way. Once an incident occurred which changed his life completely. He used to commute by train from Serampore to Khidiripur where he worked in an office. One day as he was going to the Serampore station to catch a train, he heard screams of distress and approached the person who was in pain and suffering. His heart was filled with compassion, and forgetting all about his office he took the man in his lap and attended him. He felt a great change within him as if he heard someone whispering to him, "serving poor and needy means serving to God, and it is your duty for the rest of your life".

Mahavatar Babaji lit. 'Great Avatar (Revered) Father') is the name given to his guru by Indian Yogi Yogiraj Lahiri Mahasaya (1828-1895), and several of his disciples, who reportedly appeared to them between 1861 and 1985, as described in various publications and biographies. According to Yogananda's autobiography, Babaji has resided for at least hundreds of years in the remote Himalayan regions of India, seen in person by only a small number of disciples and others.

Mahavatar Babaji meditating in the lotus position – a drawing from *Autobiography of a Yogi*, commissioned by Paramahansa Yogananda and based on his own meeting with Babaji.

Sri Yukteswar Giri (also written Sriyuktesvara, Sri Yukteshwar) (10 May 1855 - 9 March 1936) is the monastic name of Priya Nath Karar (also spelled as Priya Nath Karada and Preonath Karar), an Indian monk and yogi, and the guru of Paramhansa Yogananda and Swami Satyananda Giri. Born in Serampore, West Bengal, Sri Yukteswar was a Kriya yogi, a Jyotisha (Vedic astrologer), a scholar of the Bhagavad Gita and the Upanishads, an educator, author, and astronomer. He was a disciple of Lahiri Mahasaya of Varanasi and a member of the *Giri* branch of the Swami order. As a guru, he had two ashrams, one in Serampore and another in Puri, Odisha, between which he alternated his residence throughout the year as he trained disciples.

Paramahansa Yogananda (born Mukunda Lal Ghosh; January 5, 1893 – March 7, 1952) was an Indian Hindu monk, yogi and guru who introduced millions to the teachings of meditation and Kriya Yoga through his organization Self-Realization Fellowship (SRF) / Yogoda Satsanga Society (YSS) of India, and who lived his last 32 years in America. A chief disciple of the Bengali yoga guru Swami Sri Yukteswar Giri, he was sent by his lineage to spread the teachings of yoga to the West, to prove the unity between Eastern and Western religions and to preach a balance between Western material growth and Indian spirituality. His long-standing influence in the American yoga movement, and especially the yoga culture of Los Angeles, led him to be considered by yoga experts as the "Father of Yoga in the West.

www.ingramcontent.com/pod-product-compliance
Lightning Source LLC
Chambersburg PA
CBHW050604160726
48003CB00003B/1047